Caught in the Light

poems by

Layle Keane Chambers

Finishing Line Press
Georgetown, Kentucky

Caught in the Light

for my son

ACKNOWLEDGMENTS

The following is a list of the poems in the chapbook that have been published in
various literary journals.

Last Seen" appeared in *Collateral's* Spring 2023 Issue 7.2.
"Snapshot" appeared in the *Middle West Press Anthology, The Things We Carry Still*
(Fall 2023).
"Ceremony" and "a day without fear" appeared in the *Red Noise Collective Winter
2023 Journal.*
"D.U.S.T.W.U.N." appears in *Proud to Be: Writing by American Warriors*, vol. 13
(Southeastern Missouri State University Press).
"Caught in the Light of Currents" was published in *The Poetry Society of South
Carolina Yearbook 2025*
"Becoming a Lighthouse #1," "you find wonders," and "Pilot Air" appeared in the
March 2025 issue of *The Wrath Bearing Tree Literary Magazine*
"Ascension, the force that lifts" was published by *Line of Advance Literary Journal* in
September 2025

Publisher: Leah Huete de Maines
Editor: Christen Kincaid
Cover Art: Layle Keane Chambers
Back Cover Art: Barbara Banthien
Author Photo: Deborah B. Gilbert
Cover Design: Elizabeth Maines McCleavy

Order online: www.finishinglinepress.com
also available on amazon.com

Author inquiries and mail orders:
Finishing Line Press
PO Box 1626
Georgetown, Kentucky 40324
USA

Contents

"Everyone has oceans to fly, if they have the heart to do it.
Is it reckless? Maybe. But what do dreams know of boundaries?"

—Amelia Earhart

"Are you scared? Well, don't you worry, honey.
If they could get a washing machine to fly,
my Jimmy could land it."

—the character of Blanche Lovell
as played by Jean Speegle Howard in *Apollo 13*

The Door

I hear him, my son, my child,
my heart moving in his room
six steps away

not knowing if he has slept
waiting for word from
a military academy

I distrust

Walking with him
last summer, smell of pines
"end of the line for you, ma'am"

He turned once before
following the winding blacktop
up the hill without me

counting breaths, I wait
sun filtering through
the shutters I love

in this house we bought
together, you eleven sitting
in the title office

now you lie in bed
and look at the hole
you put in the wall and wait

for what? to check, again?
I trust you, baby! I trust your instinct
not an institution built on exclusion

the dust shifts in the warming air
I hear the dog breathing
at the side of my bed

the morning slowly becomes the day
that will change your life, I let
my eyes close, release the breath

I hold

the moment, the space of
an exhale and then an in
as our world changes seasons

I hear the six steps
stop, wait on the tile
outside my room, email

pulled up on the laptop
you've left on your bed blaring
disqualified in the subtle dawn

my stomach dropping, pooling
between hip bones where I
dredge to answer questions

in your eyes, thinking
you are not good enough
when I know you are better

each step one closer
to finding out
what it means

to fly

Ceremony

I want a hangar bare

don't dare ask
me to speak

look me dead
in the eye
to hand

the flag

don't let
your gaze
land

on the ground

S.E.R.E.D*

They train him for torture
the last call leaves Brecht
rising in my gut

> watch him grow, celebrate twenty-four
> send him off to war where it is said
> they will call for their mothers

>> my son
Survived fatherless
Evaded bitterness
Resisted hate, and
Escaped whole and perfect

What more could the Air Force want?

> framed by fireplace
> forearms beginning to bulge
> camo pants. *I want to be a pilot, mom*

Now terrorized
by a retired Navy SEAL, been in twenty years and
determined to make it real, to make my son feel
like he is an enemy and will never sit in his sunroom again

*Survival, Evasion, Resistance, Escape, and Done!

What I Did When I Could Do Nothing

red edged   flowed out
to find you
boxed   celled   somehow kept
and I felt   useful

> *of some use to you*

gazed into   tendency
strained and bit
back turned   against the wind
wide open ran

> *but that won't help*

pour the milk   soften
and   swallow, somehow stand
the dust is here, the dish and cup
the dog on the walk

ears up and pressing on
I kneel to pick a goat head
out of love, out of need, out of crying out
what do I do? while you are doing

> *do we need you broken?*

and did I sign up, too?
I don't remember
agreeing to hold my breath
pluck hairs, stare into the blue

> *no, they don't want us grieving*

mother-love immobilized, panic in its place
but the world is unhelped by helplessness, so
gather and bind to us   the air
a letter you sent, favored rock, flattened coin

choke
knowing you won't eat tonight
read   the Geneva Conventions
imagine   surfing

Becoming a Lighthouse #1

cold laps the shore
no choice but to step in
stride out, stake my place
transmute into tower

two minutes since last I looked
no longer 12:59 now 1:01
I count the difference between
my night and your morning

losing you on the Caspian Sea
where signal ends and I
set my clock to wake when
you are expected to land

how should I feel
when you are flying over
Turkmenistan?

I make my feet melt
into bedrock, desire me
into mortar and stone

I strobe the
surface of the earth

I send a beacon
to your soul

should it be jolted free

then you send pictures of the Hindu Kush
mountains I will never see

On the Ground

how I still protect you

        how
     I learn
each place
on earth
you go

     walk googlemaps
     searching

a shop
a   café
that   looks good

if lucky with streetview

the yellow-person
lands in Tallinn, Tel-Aviv, Guam
greyed out in Guantanamo
and Al Udeid is just

               dirt

drop in
on a road
closest blue
South Graham or Medicine Lake
outside barracks at Fairchild
watching while
you were at S.E.R.E.

stared six hours   satellite view
X-shaped structure on
Survival Loop

   wondering which
building, base, black-top
airfield, wide strip of asphalt
I zoom
each place

I learn
50 bucks a month
global service
     on your phone

a text at

     12:59 am
     ███████
     I love you

  over the ocean

thank god for Gander

     we made up an acronym
     predictive text has memorized
     otg means

Call me when you are

oh,

and if you take a left leaving Sinbad's Hotel & Suites
you'll find a Tim Hortons at the end of the street

Snapshot

my lockscreen
you
suited up
strapped into
cockpit, T-6 Texan
masked and tubed to fight
first solo flight
$ ride

the morning
strums
face fear
practice
Like sit ups
Like a fist
beneath belly flesh
iron

Mwanangu/My Son in Swahili

1.

       skirt the Red Sea
cruise thirty thousand feet over the
Necropolis-Luxor-Aswan-Khartoum
still familiar names   then
Boma, Kidepo, Gulu   into Entebbe

google:
'most dangerous place in the world'
    relieved Caracas came up
Uganda, landlocked Africa
foreigners are *mzungu,*
2.196 on the peace index

2.

I discover the peace index
   a world flat on the Mercator map
      colors range purple to deep orange
       Canada's indigo invites

Uganda not much different than the U.S.
a few decimals, point two but close   to Kenya
where Henry 'Mitch' Mayfield Jr. died
on Sunday January 5th, 2020 I was

driving home after visiting you in Altus
when al-Shabaab ambushed Manda Bay
newspaper said his mother, Carmoneta,
was nervous   so close to Somalia

3.

In Uganda there is a gorilla sanctuary
Bwindi's impenetrable mud and green
Mount Stanley snowcapped far
from the attack in Niger   October 4th, 2017

Bryan Black, Jeremiah Johnson, Dustin Wright
finally   announcing the fourth fatality   not clear
whether he had been captured and killed
or separated during the fight   La David T. Johnson

4.

the president told Myeshia
he knew what he signed up for

5.

The president called to offer America's
condolences
kept calling him 'your guy', *kijana wako*
but I know he was *mpenzi wako*, your love

6.

I hit listen on google translate, to hear
my son spoken in Swahili again
to learn makes me feel better

7.

The Rwenzori Mountains will be to your right
as you descend, left as you leave, I wish you could see
Murchison Falls but I'm sure there is no
time to see the elephants

Uruk

Aramaic incantation bowls
spiral words to capture
demons under doors

you send me pictures from the
Mesopotamian Alluvial Plain
where words began

where Balad Air Base is taking fire
2 rockets crash into a dormitory and 3
into the canteen

Mission Days

1.

I bought blue Sam Edelman sandals
the night you left for Dwyer
that will remind me

I'll wear them this summer
when we walk down Meeting Street
to the Battery

always drawn toward water

not the green sliver of Helmand
River Valley

but the warm Atlantic
you are crossing

2.

I am in the pause now
caught between shores

counting hours

and the ghost base eludes
my googling

but I've gotten good
at finding you I think
I could see an airstrip
on satellite view from
orbit

but one click closer
and it's gone.

3.

my paypal worked in Landstuhl
when yours didn't, it made me
happy to buy you dinner

I thought the sunrise
you sent from Kuwait City
was sunset

I spent my night
checking windspeeds
out of Hamid Karzai International

4.

in the inbetween

you are flying
and that's all I can ask

because I am not
being handed a folded flag

I see the mothers and
young wives at podiums
and I wonder

how is it they can speak?

they are not strong or stoic
they are shattered

and inviolable

Egress

This is how it feels
to lose a war
a shoe left in the street

the child's eye
haunting the photograph
one day before disaster

I know you want to be
in it
reaching out
to grasp
the man's hand

that ran up
on the ramp
and asked you
for a death

he'd rather have
than what's coming
when you depart

the access
and egress
of Kabul

seared on your skin
but you are training
in Oklahoma

and I spend
the morning
in absolution

Becoming a Lighthouse #2

Each ocean crossing
takes one day from me

each landing gives it back

even—ing out on the dark
ocean night, where the time
to PNR = E x H / (O + H)*

sleepless solidarity
navigating continents
faint green light

my two sides/hope
and despair time stamped
zero one hundred zulu

I set my clock to wake, to send
a text that you won't get but
when you land you'll see

I was awake and watching
I was over Greenland

listening to Danish ATC, hands
grazing controls, alert
as the earth curved

and the sun rose

muscle strengthened
being stretched

*E – Endurance   H – Returning Groundspeed
  O = Proceeding Groundspeed

Caught in the Light of Currents

I know what's coming when I catch my son
checking the weather in Ukraine
(or Doha, or Djibouti)
so I settle in

I ask Alexa
what are the points of stars called?
she answers "the points of stars are called points"

I am reminded to call things what they are

being scared
is uncomfortable
like walking barefoot
on this January sand
the cold burns
but doesn't   hurt

as I step now
we are alive

Vector

I didn't know
then but know
now

I was afraid
you would fly
the fighter

so I set a table
for fear to
gather

placeholder for each
graceholder
place to remember

how close I hold bitter
herb and grace o'Sundays
salt and still water

I sit down
with othersides
and the halfhour before

your topstick decision
makes this choice

not the other

A 'vector' is a heading or direction given by Air Traffic Control to guide an aircraft's flight path. After the primary phase of specialized training, student pilots in the Air Force are selected for one of three advanced training tracks or 'vectors' based on the needs of the Air Force and their class standing.

Snapshot

the act of vigil
   is connection
     between
   looked for
and looker

you were 13
when I let go

& let you fly
while I
still had some say
now I
stand the watch

Ascension, the force that lifts

I lay await in blue claire sleep
suspended stilled readiness

text ding 2:53 am *test* (to see if it got to me)
I respond *yes!* with an emoji heart

Amelia's voice in my head *'everyone has oceans to fly...'*
and I can't sleep when you are

you tried to call   no go   too far
too on the otherside   I pick up

silence

I follow the signs and calculate times,
lines and gather, but it's as if different rules

are played, as if I can cradle in my two palms
lift and throw to the air four winded

where I stand burst open in that bookstore
where I found the Earhart quote

where I look up and wonder
where is ASCN 1ZZ

island of no indigenous peoples
sheered from the South Atlantic

a damn rock in the middle of the ocean
nothing romantic—

just another place for man to step
on his way to somewhere else

where you tried to call
while in the act of rising

you find wonders

I'm glad you broke in Aqaba not Benghazi
resort style hotel, manmade island
with security

your voice uneasy wanting to be home for thanksgiving
stranded, describing the intense blue green
of the Red Sea

shards of unsaid stuck in my hand

then your pilot eyes find the nearest wonder
and you walk me
to Petra

where a rose canyon gives you
tea to drink in a cave and I see
the men who made it

rozmazać>rōz-ma-zache>blur

you say 'landed—in Europe'
but I know it's Poland
zoom in on green
and grey rectangles

runways to hold
all you carry
droga startowa>
d-r long oh-ga star-t long oh-va

I fall asleep wet hair
break the bedside glass
reaching for a text
I missed   get up, run hard
in rain—envision

a descent on Rzeszów>*zheh-shaaf*
Jasionka>*jay-ʒunka*, rolling the final
for droga startova 09/27
jay-town on the outstretched plain

my mouth learns soft sounds
I read the sixteen things
I don't know about Poland

arching the tongue is one

to say Szczecin>*steh-cheen*
or Oswiecim>*ow-shvayn-chm*
gathering language that speaks
for the stones in my throat

Last Seen

I saw my son near Bangor ME, near St. John's
near Keflavik and Faroe
climbing a bolted route through clouds
I saw my son body surfing Folly between tides
soaking in the homelight

I saw my son as a green line on a computer screen
    ending at 1:46 am

in the shock of 21 guns
kneeling to offer
packing his bag again

I saw my son crying in the shadow
    of the clocktower
finding the deep water of the stroke
I saw my son near Farranfore, 4:56 UCT
two-fisted, lifting the weight
    of a man who was father to him

I saw my son sipping scotch in a Glasgow pub
twisted in the canal
waving from the porch

I saw him grieve a dream, un-gnarl history
wear an open-heart t-shirt
float a feather in the upstream
in his driveway, in his Jeep

in Tallinn, in Landstuhl
in Rzeszow, in Constanta
on Strada Tudor Vladimirescu
near the Black, Caspian, Baltic Sea

I saw my son nearing Cartwright, Canada
    on this side of the world again
I saw him
check his phone

the Day day

I.
will this be the one I replay?
if so, I better pay attention

II.
Cut a camellia
and put it in a blue
sea glass vase

a shade so subtle I cry halfway
between cream and pink

III.
your ringtone and everything—the world, the dog
even the cat stops

can we come over tonight, mom
be together?

a quick finger count off
18 hours starting

                        now

IV.
Buy wine and local shrimp
at Crosby's, contemplate Old Bay

more attracted to the can than
what's inside

you can't drink because
you're sitting Bravo

but we talk

while I enjoy my Kitchen Sink
White Blend with citrus notes
Devein and clean—shrimp so fresh
it still has seagrass clinging

you finish a second Black Cherry Seltzer
I toss the salad with fresh ground
pepper and sweetheart grape
tomatoes

you start the grill because I've forgotten
how many things you do for me

was this the night we played the question game?
was this the night we watched another episode
of the show we only watch when we're together?

pennywort and wild violets
beneath our feet as we walk the dogs

I go to sleep hearing you
and your wife laughing
until twisted at four am when
the alarm rings and you are
up half dressed
in the dark

say 'bye, love you
like it's any other day

V.
I drive for hours
to understand what it means
to say "*I need to go*"

I mean, he'll be
a grizzled old colonel
someday, right?

(reader pauses)

right?

(reader pauses again)

the   same   text
over and over
must be bouncing towers

otg in MK

Mauritius, Macedonia
former Republic of Yugoslavia
not ML, thank you angels
no, not a country, an airport code
the ICAO is LRCK

so close
the Black Sea

VI.
how will I sleep
on your fifth or sixth crossing
in as many days?

It's been
more hours than you
need—

then

> *getting a shower, mom*
> *will try to sleep a bit*
> *love you, take care.*

VII.
I know he and I are looking at the same sky.

VIII.
don't stop me while I'm dancing

                         while I've got my earbuds in
while I'm understanding
                and notice
that buds are beginning to show
on the ends of my fingers

Pilot Air

A.I.B. and
consequent
articles
lead off:

pilot error

so easy

to say, slips so
easy off

so
easy
off the side
nose over tail

so easy
to say: who knows?

what happens

in the air
where

when thinking fails
there is training
when training fails
there is sky
when sky fails
there is

g r o u n d

The Color of Khartoum

What will I color
Sudan on the calendar
April 18th until an undisclosed
day in the future

SRD sounds nice
soft return date

unvocalized
sibilance and fricative
gentle landing

on the lips, soft return

but the date? hard *d* and *t*
is their way of not telling me
when you'll be back

what will I write
instead of Sudan
(where you can't tell me

but I know you're going)

I color Sudan bright yellow
and call it your smile

I choreograph a dance
and name it Sudan

I sing Sudan
like a lullaby

Me: *Are we going to think about this?*
The Other Me *(stupid one): Yes, I guess. It can't hurt. Right?*

a day without fear

Where is he now? What is he doing? These are the thoughts that
fill the time. Sleeping. Eating. Flying. The islands below. That one
looks like a dog chasing a bird. Thin clouds slip like sheets over the
fuselage, making a sound that is almost like sucking in a breath.

Last night they knocked. She always imagined they would ring
the bell. But the knock came quiet, whispered, in the distance. She
strained to hear and, curious, approached the door. The shadow of
shoulders past the peep hole. The tide rose and took her under in
the softness of a wave. Evening Blue had always been her favorite
Crayola color, and now, here it was. All over. She didn't get angry,
as she had also imagined, and refuse them entrance. No. She let
them in.

Now no questions.

D.U.S.T.W.U.N.

(Duty Status Whereabouts Unknown, a.k.a. the parts of a pop song)

I need to know
where you are
even when I don't

even when I can't
when intelligence concerns
are greater than a mother's

I need to know
where your body
is on this earth

where the body
come from mine is
circling urban centers

where you turn vague
where I am just sitting
soaking wet

living the rivulets
swimming in cold
September water

"this is it, Mom"
                       "ok"
"I love you, goodbye"

I love you   the verse
goodbye   the bridge

24, 34, 38 hours
growing fears
and a widening war

Was it this day? —not this day
with ripe pineapple and Boursin
cheese on olive toast

a minus zero morning
and startled blackcrown
night herons

Ali Al Salem screen cast
to the TV—flight line, fingers
Quarry, Rock, Billabong quarter

back out to view
a bigger picture first
and second desert storms

I love you   refrain
goodbye   the hook

not that day
when the sun
caught your hand

still waving too far
down the road where
I stood and watched the hawk

awhile
before I got keys
unable to sit

in the feeling, not the day
when the Wapoo
turned metal

a skiff carved silver
silence of winter on water
—not today

where
I will be
here

where you will be
where spirals shut down
where I lose your signal

I love you   the chorus
goodbye   the break

I wanted you to be a poet
you wanted to be a pilot

now it's tomorrow
where you are
and I sit

by an ocean

Becoming a Lighthouse #3

rehearsing, I stand
spinning green lines
and ghost light gestures

at the end of my island

Morris bides
brick and white stripes
no longer alert

the water the light and tides
a pelican formation flyby
the comings and going

shift to cycle
dune grass waves
wait

I am content

to watch
to walk out
to the abutment

sketch my feelings
on sand to show you
someday

when
mission done
white caps wash

Layle Keane Chambers is a performing poet, advocate, and proud Air Force mom living in Folly Beach, South Carolina. Her work is driven by a singular mission: to strip away the exposition of life and speak in the most essential terms. She believes that poetry allows us to connect to one another through an emotional bond that goes beyond a purely intellectual one.

Born into a life of movement—from Detroit, Colorado, and Texas to Japan, Germany, and London—to NYC's East Village in the 1980s, Layle's perspective is uniquely global yet deeply personal. With twenty years of experience as an educator and a background as an Artistic Director in theatre, she has spent her career helping others find power in their own narratives.

Currently serving as the Vice President of the Poetry Society of South Carolina, Layle focuses her lens on the often-unseen realities of military families. Her debut collection, *Caught in the Light*, embraces the unfiltered truths of her journey to becoming a pilot's mom. Through stark and intimate verse, it captures the breathtaking beauty and ever-present anxiety inherent in the world of aviation and military service. She is also the co-author of *Glass: Gather. Engage. Give.*, a guide to preparedness and inner strength.

Layle remains dedicated to speaking the sublime and difficult, and to a mission of bringing indescribable states of human experience into the light.

Connect with her online: Layle Keane Chambers, author (Facebook), @laylethewhale (Instagram), @laylekeanechambers (Substack), and on LinkedIn at Layle Chambers

www.ingramcontent.com/pod-product-compliance
Lightning Source LLC
Chambersburg PA
CBHW020219090426

42734CB00008B/1142